ISBN 978-0-331-38723-0
PIBN 11116329

Historic, archived document

Do not assume content reflects current
scientific knowledge, policies, or practices.

FAMILY ECONOMICS REVIEW

Consumer and Food Economics Research Division,   Agricultural Research Service,

UNITED STATES DEPARTMENT OF AGRICULTURE

A quarterly report on current developments in family and food economics and economic aspects of home management, prepared for home demonstration agents and home economics specialists of the Cooperative Extension Service.

ANNUAL OUTLOOK ISSUE

CONTENTS

ARS 62-5
December 1963   Washington, D.C.

The articles in this issue are condensa-
tions of papers presented at the 41st Annual
National Agricultural Outlook Conference,
held in Washington, D.C., November 18-21,
1963.

Reference to any trade name does not constitute an endorsement by the U.S.
Department of Agriculture over others not mentioned.

ERRATUM: In the September 1963 issue of <u>Family Economics Review</u>, page 7,
table 3, the heading for the fourth column should be 35-44 instead of
35-64.

NATIONAL ECONOMIC SITUATION AND OUTLOOK FOR 1964

Rex F. Daly
Economic and Statistical Analysis Division

Economic activity has increased at a brisk pace so far in 1963. Demand
expansion was rather broadly based, with increases in consumer buying and a
continued rise in outlays for fixed capital, construction activity, and Government purchases of goods and services. Rising incomes, strong markets for
autos, and further increases in business capital outlays and Government purchases promise continued expansion in business activity in the months ahead.

The economy is buoyant and the outlook is favorable for 1964. But the
course and vigor of economic activity in 1964 will depend to a considerable
extent on the size and timing of the proposed tax cut. A reduction in tax
rates such as that passed by the House of Representatives and under considera-
tion in the Senate, would add about $6 billion to the flow of consumer dis-
posable income in 1964. Such an addition to aftertax income would step up consumer demand and, subsequently, investment demands of business as well. The
outlook for 1964 also assumes a somewhat slower rise in Federal Government expenditures, no material change in the international situation, and increased
exports of farm products to Communist-bloc countries.

Consumer Markets.--Rising consumer incomes supplemented by increased use
of installment credit financed a substantial advance in consumer purchases of
goods and services this year. Consumer incomes after taxes in the third
quarter of 1963 were at an annual rate more than 4.5 percent higher than a
year earlier. The increase of nearly 5 percent in consumer spending was
broadly based: Outlays for services increased 6 percent, nondurable goods
nearly 4 percent, and durable goods 6 percent above third quarter 1962 rates.
Automobile sales played a key role in increased sales of durable goods. Consumers also substantially increased their purchases of furniture and appliances, general merchandise, gasoline, food, and services such as rent and
household operation, transportation, and personal care.

The flow of income to consumers is expected to continue to increase. A
reduction in tax rates early in 1964 would accelerate the rise in the after-
tax income of consumers. Higher incomes would step up consumer purchases of
goods and services. Such demand increases would not only lead directly to increases in output, but probably also to a step-up in demand for fixed investment and business inventories. Accordingly, the increase in consumer disposable income and consumer buying could well exceed gains over the past year.
Surveys of consumer buying plans indicate a continued high level of purchases
of autos and other durable goods.

Investment Demand.--Gross investment outlays, which include business
fixed capital outlays, new construction, and inventories in total, have risen
strongly since the first quarter of 1963. Outlays for new plant and equipment
are expected to rise further in coming months.

New construction activity has increased this year, with residential housing starts up to around 1.6 million units in the third quarter from 1.4 million a year earlier. Residential construction activity is expected to continue high in the coming year.

Net additions to inventories in 1963 were about in line with the expansion in sales and economic activity. If price advances are moderate during 1964, inventory policy is expected to remain conservative with net additions to inventory about in line with increases in final demands.

Government Expenditures.--Expenditures for goods and services by Federal, State, and local governments were at an annual rate of $126 billion in the third quarter, $9 billion above a year earlier. Revenues have risen slightly more than expenditures. The increase in Government purchases in the coming year may not match the $9 billion annual increase over the third quarter 1962. Recent discussion relating to commitments in defense and space activities emphasizes efforts to maintain a tight rein on increases in Federal expenditures.

Output, Employment, and Prices.--Output of factories and mines in the third quarter 1963 was at a rate 6 percent above a year earlier. Increases over the year were fairly general, reflecting the expanded demand for autos, household appliances, food, apparel, and other consumer goods. Increased purchases by business and Government resulted in increased output of capital goods and defense materials.

Nonagricultural employment in the third quarter was at a rate of 64 million, a gain of 1.2 million from a year earlier; farm employment continued its gradual downtrend. The number of job seekers entering the labor force continued to rise, and the unemployment rate held relatively stable at a little above 5.5 percent of the labor force. Reductions in unemployment, however, have taken place among married men. Unemployment rates continue highest among workers who lack experience and training.

Real output of the economy, such as industrial production, farm output, and construction, was at a rate in the third quarter about 4 percent above a year earlier. Total employment increased around 1.5 percent and the length of the work week held fairly stable at a high level. The implied rise in output per man-hour of around 2.5 percent is about in line with average annual increases since the mid-1950's. Average hourly earnings in manufacturing in the third quarter were 2.8 percent above a year earlier.

The increase in output over the past year did not exert much upward pressure on prices. The Consumer Price Index continued to creep up--around 1 percent--due in large measure to rising prices for services.

Expanding demands on the economy are expected to lead to further increases in output and employment in the coming year. With the proposed tax cut, gains would be large enough to bring about some improvement in the overall unemployment rate as the year progresses. Since some major industries are producing somewhat below preferred operating rates, no great price pressure is indicated.

Wage rates will continue to rise in the coming year. Expected increases in employment would expand personal incomes more than the gain of 4.5 percent over the past year. A reduction in tax rates would likely accelerate the gain in the after-tax income of consumers. Expanding economic activity will increase off-farm employment opportunities for farm people.

† FOOD †

Stephen J. Hiemstra
Economic and Statistical Analysis Division

Food prices in 1963 are averaging about 1.5 percent above last year's level. This rise is somewhat greater than in recent years. Charges per unit for processing and marketing foods originating on U.S. farms rose 4 percent during 1963, about twice the average rate of increase in the last decade. Average retail prices of food from livestock products in 1963 are down slightly from 1962. Prices of food from crops are up by 3 or 4 percent, due partly to Florida's freeze-damage and high sugar prices. Prices of food purchased and consumed away from home are up 2.5 percent. The total price increase for all food slightly exceeds the average rise in the Consumer Price Index (all commodities and services) so far in 1963, in contrast to the more usual case of the CPI going up more than its food component.

During 1964, retail food prices may creep upward but the rise is expected to be less than the increase in 1963. Retail prices of food from livestock products are expected to average about the same as in 1963. Some upward price pressure may develop on foods from crops, as was the case in 1963. Further increases can be expected in prices of food consumed in restaurants and other away-from-home eating places.

Total food consumption in 1963 is up about 2 percent from last year (price-weighted index). Since population is up about 1.5 percent, per capita food consumption is up about half of 1 percent. Even though this sounds like a small increase, it is the largest since 1959. Since 1947-49, per capita food consumption has increased a total of only 4 percent.

In 1963, red meat consumption per capita is totaling about 170 pounds, carcass equivalent, up 4 percent from 1962. Most of this increase is in beef, up an estimated 7 percent to a record 95 pounds per capita. Consumption in the final quarter of the year is expected to be up sharply. Veal and lamb consumption are both down from last year. Pork consumption is up about 1 pound to 65 pounds, but is running below year-earlier rates in the final months of the year.

The outlook for 1964 is for total meat consumption per capita to remain near 1963 levels. Some further rise may occur in beef consumption, but no repeat of 1963's sharp increase is in prospect. Pork consumption may be down slightly from 1963.

Broiler consumption per capita in 1963 is up slightly, but turkey consumption is about steady. In total, poultry consumption is slightly larger for the year, and a further small increase is foreseen for 1964. Per capita egg consumption is down by 2 or 3 percent. Production in the winter months is expected to run ahead of the year-earlier period, but the 1964 outlook is for per capita consumption to continue near the 1963 level.

Fish consumption is down in 1963. Despite lower fish landings, lower imports, and higher exports, cold storage stocks on October 1 were 8 percent larger than a year earlier.

Per capita consumption of all dairy products in 1963 is holding about steady with last year's level. Some declines are occurring in per capita consumption of fluid whole milk and cream, condensed and evaporated milk, and cottage cheese. But they are being offset by increases in consumption of other cheese, ice cream, fluid skim milk, and nonfat dry milk. In 1964, little change is expected in consumption per capita of total dairy products, but further shifts may occur among dairy products.

In the first 9 months of 1963, retail prices of livestock products were generally steady to lower than in the same months of 1962. An exception was egg prices, up 3 percent. Meat and chicken prices normally decline in the final months of the year. This year's decline for meat may be more than seasonal because of unusually large supplies. The outlook for 1964 is for retail prices of livestock products to average about the same as in 1963. However, there may be some price declines for beef, eggs, and other products expected to be in large supply.

In 1963, consumption per capita of fats and oils is running a little below 1962. Further declines are taking place for animal fats; lard and butter are both down. Consumption of margarine is up slightly but consumption of salad and cooking oils is down from 1962. The outlook for 1964 is for per capita consumption of total fats and oils to remain about steady with 1963's 45.5 pounds (fat content). Consumption of vegetable oils may increase and animal fats decline further.

Fruit consumption is down rather sharply in 1963, mostly because of the freeze damage to citrus fruit. Both fresh and processed fruit consumption are down, but fresh and frozen items are down more than canned fruit. Canned fruit juice consumption is up, largely as a result of an increase in pineapple juice used extensively in fruit drinks. Dried fruit consumption is running ahead of 1962. Some recovery is in prospect for consumption of fresh fruit next year. Citrus consumption likely will increase a little but is expected to remain well below levels of recent years because of tree damage. The consumption of canned fruits and all juices is expected to decline below that of 1963. Tree nut consumption is much greater this year than last. Pecan supplies are at record-large volume after last year's short crop.

Per capita consumption of vegetables in 1963 is running about the same as last year. Slight declines in fresh consumption are being offset by modest increases in processed items, particularly frozen vegetables. Fresh tomato consumption is down, but tomato juice is up. The outlook for 1964 is for stability of consumption in fresh vegetables and some slight rise in processed vegetables. Potato consumption in 1963 is running slightly above 1962 because of increased use of processed potatoes, but sweetpotato consumption is down slightly. No change in consumption of potatoes is expected in 1964.

Wheat flour and other cereal product consumption per capita in 1963 is about steady with 1962. Total supply of food grains continues to exceed domestic food use by a large margin. No important changes are foreseen for 1964.

A fractional rise in per capita consumption of sugars and sirups combined is taking place in 1963. Per capita consumption of corn sirup is rising about 4 percent, and corn sugar is rising about 7 percent. But use of these items is minor compared with cane and beet sugar. Next year's consumption of sugars and sirups combined is expected to be about steady with 1963.

Reduced supplies of fruits and certain vegetables caused average retail prices of all fruits and vegetables to rise 6 percent in the first 9 months of 1963 compared with the same months of 1962. Sugar and sweets averaged 8 percent higher. Cereal and bakery product prices were up 2 percent. In the final months of the year, prices of fruits are expected to decline seasonally but remain well above year-earlier levels. No repeat of 1963's unusual supply conditions for foods from crops is anticipated for 1964. But some selective increases may occur in prices of foods that have trended upward during the past decade. Further price increases can be expected in processed fruits whose stocks are being reduced in 1963.

Summary.--The 1964 outlook for food consumption per capita is for continuation at about this year's level. Retail food prices likely will continue their long-term upward trend, but the rise will be less than occurred in 1963.

CLOTHING

Virginia Britton
Consumer and Food Economics Research Division

Clothing consumption, prices, and supplies are overall about the same this year as last year: Per capita expenditure for clothing has changed little; consumer prices for apparel are at about the same level; and supplies of clothing and raw materials are high. At the same time, noteworthy changes are occurring in clothing as research and development continue apace toward improving the end use properties of materials.

Clothing consumption.--Aggregate expenditure for clothing and shoes in the United States continued to climb in 1962, but increases in the population and in prices meant that there was little change in the real value (in constant dollars) of clothing purchased per person, based on Department of Commerce figures. In fact, from 1955 to 1962 there was a difference of only 4 percent between the highest and lowest average annual value per person. Clothing and shoes took about 8 percent of disposable personal income in 1962, as they did in the past 6 years.

A comparison of urban expenditures in 1950 and 1960 in studies made by the Bureau of Labor Statistics shows trends in family clothing expenditures similar to those shown by the aggregate figures just discussed. The surveys indicated that urban families (including single consumers) spent for clothing, materials, and services an average of $549 in 1960 compared with $437 in 1950-- an increase of 11 percent in constant dollars. The increase in real income, however, was greater than this. Consequently, the share of income taken by clothing decreased. The relevant preliminary data may be summarized as follows:

	1950	1960	Percent increase
Current dollars:			
Money income after taxes	3,910	5,822	48.9
Clothing, materials, and services .	437	549	25.6
Clothing as percent of income ...	11.2	9.4	--
1960 dollars:			
Money income after taxes	4,829	5,822	20.6
Clothing, materials, and services .	494	549	11.1
Clothing as percent of income ...	10.2	9.4	--

Another source of information on clothing expenditures is the current judgment of retailers. Trade reports this fall are that clothing is selling well, with a general upgrading of purchases: Higher-priced lines in women's and men's clothing, stylish imports including Italian ready-to-wear clothes, high-fashion items such as fake fur and metallic fabrics in women's apparel, an emphasis on "dressing up" for occasions, and the "sportive" look in sportswear.

Consumer prices.--There has been almost no change in the level of prices of clothing over the past year as measured by the Apparel Index of the Bureau of Labor Statistics. (See table.) From September 1962 to September 1963, this index rose only 0.2 percent. In the same period the Consumer Price Index for all items rose 0.9 percent. In 1961 and 1962 also the Apparel Index rose less than the all-items index.

Price movements among the apparel subgroups are usually not parallel and the past year has been no exception in this respect. The index for women's and girls' apparel fell 1 percent from September 1962 to September 1963, while the indexes for men's and boys' apparel and for footwear increased 1 percent.

These changes are in line with price movements in recent years. Since 1960,
either men's and boys' apparel or footwear has led the price increase.

Increase in selected indexes of consumer prices

Index	1960 to 1961	1961 to 1962	September 1962 to September 1963
	Percent	Percent	Percent
Consumer Price Index	1.1	1.2	0.9
Apparel Index	.7	.4	.2
Mens' and boys' apparel	1.2	.5	1.2
Women's and girls' apparel ..	.3	-.1	-1.1
Footwear	.9	1.4	1.1
Other apparel	-.4	-.3	.2
Cotton apparel	.5	.7	.8
Wool apparel	1.1	.2	2.1
Manmade fibers apparel	.2	.1	.3

Source: Bureau of Labor Statistics.

    Grouping clothing by fiber explains some of the movement in the type
groups. From September 1962 to September 1963, prices of cotton apparel rose
0.8 percent, wool apparel rose 2.1 percent, and apparel of manmade fibers rose
0.3 percent. Among these subgroups, cotton apparel led the price advance in
1962 and wool apparel led in 1961.

    Prices of clothing are subject to some seasonal fluctuations--changes
which recur regularly at certain times of the year. A recent study by BLS
puts into numerical terms the size of these seasonal fluctuations in price
series for apparel and apparel subgroups, as well as for about 85 other consumer price series.

    Among the four apparel subgroups, the seasonal fluctuation of retail
prices is greatest for women's and girls' apparel. In fact, fluctuation in
this subgroup plays a primary role in the seasonal variation of the all-apparel
group. In the seasonal pattern for women's and girls' apparel, the year's low
point is in January and there is a spring peak in March, followed by a downward drift through the summer. Prices start to climb in September to the year's
peak in October, then there is a downward slide. Men's and boys' apparel and
"other apparel" also show a tendency to rise to a fall peak. Footwear, on the
other hand, shows no meaningful seasonal pattern. Because of the differences

among the four subgroups, seasonal fluctuation in prices of all apparel is only about half as great as that for women's and girls' apparel.

Seasonal fluctuations are important in only two of the other seven major categories of expenditure--food and transportation. Because there are off-setting seasonal fluctuations in the major categories, the all-items index of the Consumer Price Index shows no important seasonal pattern.

Developments in retail distribution of apparel.--Reports in trade sources indicate that retailers of apparel feel they need to build up present stores, especially those in downtown areas, rather than open new stores. Some increase in downtown shoe sales was noted last winter as stores focused their appeal on city dwellers rather than suburbanites in metropolitan areas. The development of shopping centers is beginning to lag after more than a decade of growth. Some areas seem to be "overstored." Branch store openings by retail chains have tapered off this year. One survey last winter showed that almost two-thirds of branch stores opened recently were performing below expectations.

Action by the Federal Trade Commission in March may have important implications for the future: The FTC ruled that a large shoe company illegally restrained competition by requiring independent franchised dealers to adhere to the company's established resale prices and to refuse to handle competing shoes from other manufacturers. The FTC ordered the company to discontinue these practices.

Supplies.--Supplies of cotton and manmade fibers are good. U.S. production of cotton in 1963 is estimated at almost 15 million bales, which is about 1 million bales more than domestic mill use and exports are expected to require. Production of manmade fibers, including textile glass fibers, increased 22 percent in 1962 over 1961, the largest one-year increase on record. Further increases are ahead as the Celanese Corporation plans to start producing nylon in the U.S. in 1964. World wool production in 1963-64 is expected to be 1 percent above last year's record high level, but U.S. mill use of apparel wool in 1963 is expected to be about 9 percent lower than last year. U.S. production of cattle hides in 1963 is expected to be the largest ever, at a time of decreased production of leather shoes.

Outlook.--Considering wholesale prices, prospective supplies and demand for raw materials, and the competition among them, there appears no strong reason to expect much further change in the near future in overall retail prices of apparel. Active competition in the development and promotion of fabrics and finishes also plays a part in this prognostication.

Further improvements in cotton garments are emerging. All-cotton stretch fabrics made into garments provide increased comfort and are being used in such articles as nurses' uniforms, blouses, sport and dress shirts, pants and slacks, corduroy garments and socks. A wash-wear treated interliner bonded to outer layers of untreated cotton in collars and cuffs of men's wash-wear shirts may result in longer service life, according to USDA research. The bonded interliner shares its wash-wear properties with the untreated cotton; and the untreated fabric offers the high resistance to fraying associated with cotton. A method for imparting wash-wear properties and at the same time permanently attaching dyes, starch, and other finishing materials to cotton in a single chemical treatment has been developed by the Southern Utilization Research and Development Division of the Agricultural Research Service.

Improvements are underway for woolen apparel and household textiles. Stretch wool fabrics are being used to provide additional comfort and better shape retention in men's suits, slacks, and jackets. Wool sweaters and blankets that can be washed by machine are appearing on the market, as are permanently pleated wool skirts and permanently creased slacks and trousers. These easy-care properties are obtained by using treatments developed by the Western Utilization Research Division and by others. The USDA shrinkproofing treatment covers wool fibers with an ultrathin coating that is chemically similar to one type of nylon. Treated wool fabrics wash with an acceptable minimum of shrinkage and retain wool's natural soft texture. This process is being used on children's clothes, skirts, and sport shirts. Suiting fabrics are just beginning to come on the market that are processed mostly by the USDA Wurlanize process. The solution used for permanent creases is applied by spraying or dipping, after which the damp fabric is steam pressed. Fabrics that have received both treatments are machine washable.

Developments are continuing in manmade fibers and fabrics. Spandex fibers that have been used in foundation garments and swimsuits are now being introduced for use in stockings for women who suffer from leg fatigue. New forms and new uses are appearing for nylon. Stretch is being added to slacks and beach wear by one form of nylon that is coiled like a spring. Fluffy texturized nylon yarns are used in sweaters. Nylon fibers with a softer feel are going into women's dresses. A type of nylon that can be molded cheaply into permanent shapes is decreasing prices of high-quality brassieres.

Nonwoven fabrics that combine the materials and production techniques of the textile and paper industries are offered for disposable bed sheets and pillowcases for hospitals. They are said to cost less than the price of laundering those made of cotton. They may be developed eventually for consumer markets.

A fluorine-based textile finish is claimed to provide oil and water repellency and stain resistance (and to retain these properties after washing and dry cleaning) without affecting the appearance or breathability of the fabric, since the finish clings to each fiber in the fabric. It is to be used first in men's and women's top-quality raincoats and outerwear, draperies, and slip covers.

Fabric shoes with plastic soles molded onto the finished uppers at a savings over the old vulcanizing method are appearing in national chain stores. A new synthetic leather, said to be a breathable shoe material, is expected to appear in men's and women's shoes in the spring of 1964. Similar synthetic products are being developed by some 20 other companies.

From the consumer's point of view, it looks like a good year ahead in the clothing area, with large supplies to meet the heavy demand, high competition among fibers, new products becoming available, and continued improvements in familiar products.

TRANSPORTATION

Lucile F. Mork
Consumer and Food Economics Research Division

Expenditures.--Expenditures for transportation, both for the purchase and operation of automobiles and for public transportation, have increased during the last decade. Part of the increase is due to higher prices, but increased ownership and use of automobiles are also important reasons for greater per person expenditures.

The Department of Commerce estimates of spending of U.S. consumers for all transportation show that in 1962 we spent 10 percent more per person than in 1961 (a sizable increase for 1 year) and 47 percent more than in 1952. During each year of this period, spending for all transportation amounted to about 12 percent of total expenditures for consumer goods and services. Purchase and operation of automobiles accounted for about 11 percent and public transportation about 1 percent.

Between 1961 and 1962, expenditures for the purchase and operation of automobiles increased more than public transportation. On a per person basis, expenditures for cars increased about 20 percent; tires, tubes, accessories and parts, and insurance about 9 percent; repairs, greasing, and washing about 4 percent; gasoline and oil about 2 percent. Expenditures for local transportation (street cars, buses, and taxis) decreased slightly, but intercity transportation increased 7 percent because of increased spending for bus and airplane travel.

The present high rate of automobile ownership is without doubt an important factor in accounting for the fact that we spend more than $1 out of every $10 for the purchase and operation of the automobile. About 4 out of 5 households have a car available for their use, according to the 1960 Census of Housing. Motor-vehicle registrations for privately owned passenger cars have more than doubled in the postwar period and increased about 50 percent in the last 10 years.

The second car has become the accepted standard in many households. In 1960, 19 percent of all households had 2 cars and 3 percent had 3 or more.

Prices.--Prices for all transportation as given in the Consumer Price Index increased only 0.1 percent last year (September 1962 to September 1963), but 20 percent in the previous 10 years (1952 to 1962). (See table.) The Consumer Price Index for all items increased 0.9 percent last year and 14 percent in the previous 10 years.

Changes in the Consumer Price Index for all items and transportation

Group and subgroup	1952 to 1962	September 1962 to September 1963
	Percent	Percent
All items	14	0.9
Transportation	20	.1
Private	15	-.2
Public	52	1.2

Source: Bureau of Labor Statistics

The slight increase last year in transportation prices was due to a 1.2 percent increase in public transportation fares. Private transportation (purchase and operation of automobiles) decreased 0.2 percent. Prices of the various goods and services included in this category did not move at the same rate or in the same direction. Used car prices increased 0.5 percent, while new cars declined 0.3 percent. Gasoline prices fell about 1 percent, repairs increased 1 percent, and tires increased about 4 percent.

Between 1952 and 1962, new car prices increased about 10 percent, after adjusting for changes in quality. Since more and more cars are equipped with such features as automatic transmission and power steering, the average price paid has, of course, increased more than this. Used car prices have fluctuated considerably in response to the tempo of the economy and reached a high in 1962. The easing of credit and the increasing number of families wanting more than one car are probably largely responsible for the current high prices of used cars.

Operating costs of automobiles also increased between 1952 and 1962. Price increases ranged from 21 percent for gasoline to 42 percent for insurance. (See chart.) Tires were the only item in the automotive group of the index that went down in price. Prices on tires fell about 7 percent.

The greatest price advance between 1952 and 1962--60 percent--was in the cost of local transit fares. Railroad fares also increased, but only 19 percent. With such a sizable increase in local transit fares, the use of local transportation declined. About half as many paying passengers used local transit lines in 1962 as in 1950.

Installment Credit.--Automobile credit has played an important part in the increase in ownership of automobiles. The average installment debt outstanding per person on automobiles was $49 in 1952 and $103 in 1962. Automobile credit accounted for about 40 percent of all installment debt in both years.

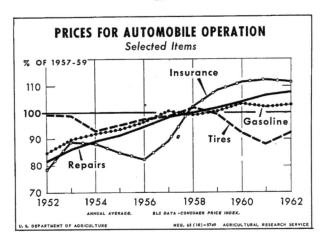

PRICES FOR AUTOMOBILE OPERATION
Selected Items

ANNUAL AVERAGE.   BLS DATA - CONSUMER PRICE INDEX.

U. S. DEPARTMENT OF AGRICULTURE   NEG. 63 (10)-5749   AGRICULTURAL RESEARCH SERVICE

About 60 percent of new passenger cars bought were bought on credit in each of the last 3 years. More car purchases plus a moderate increase in the average size of installment contracts account for most of the increase in automobile credit in 1962 and 1963. Contracts on new cars were running about 2 percent larger in early 1963 than in early 1962, and 6 percent higher than in early 1961.

List prices of new cars changed very little in the 1962 and 1963 model years, after allowing for differences in standard equipment. Consumers, however, bought more equipment--power steering and brakes--and more expensive body styles. The average size of installment contracts may have been increased also by a slight reduction in downpayments.

The average repayment period for new-car installment contracts has been gradually increasing. A larger proportion of contracts are being written at the prevailing maximum maturity of 36 months than previously. Instances in which automobile dealers and lenders have offered 42-month, and occasionally 48-month loans on new cars have been reported. On used car contracts, the repayment period has also been lengthening. The proportion with maturities of over 24 months has been increasing for several years. Many installment contracts on late-model used cars have been carrying 36-month maturities recently.

The recent extension in credit time for both new and used cars may be attributed to some extent to the extended guarantees now given by all major manufacturers. In one case, a manufacturer issues a guarantee covering the major components of the car for 5 years or 50,000 miles whichever occurs first.

Automobile Production and Sales.--The 1963 model automobile found immediate acceptance by consumers, and fourth quarter deliveries were higher in 1962 than in previous years. Sales for the first 7 months of 1963 were about 12 percent ahead of sales for the same period of 1962. Predictions are being made in industry that 1963 will be a record breaking year.

Imported cars are staging somewhat of a comeback after a 3-year downward slide. Imports reached a peak in 1959 when a record number were sold. Since that time, the number sold has decreased. Imports for the first 7 months of this year were ahead of last year for the same period.

Outlook.--The prices of 1964 models of automobiles are generally the same as for comparable 1963 models. This is in spite of price increases in labor and some basic materials that go into a car. Automobile companies point out that steel costs are up, the costs of tires are up, and labor rates are expected to go up. We may find prices raised on a few models and a few accessories. White-walled tires may go up a dollar or two, according to trade sources. Some permanent type antifreezes are expected to be priced lower than a year ago. Competition between nationally advertised and private brands is the reason behind the price reduction.

According to the U.S. Bureau of the Census, in July of this year consumers reported they expected to purchase more automobiles in the next 12 months than they did a year ago. The estimates showed a higher level of anticipated new automobile purchases than in any previous July survey in this series (1959-63). Intentions to buy used automobiles were about the same as in July 1962.

Indications point to an increase in the number of families with two or more cars. In 1964, we will have a new group of 16-year olds qualifying as drivers in many States. Some of these new drivers will work hard to convince their families that it is a good idea to have a second car. In some cases, two-car families will become three-car families.

The 1964 model automobiles are longer and flossier than the 1963 models. More models carry adjustable steering wheels, air-conditioning, and transistorized ignition systems that improve engine operations as motors get bigger and operate at faster speeds. Front seat belts will become standard equipment beginning January 1, 1964. Otherwise, differences are not too great.

Conclusion: Transportation will maintain its position of relative importance in the family budget; the supply of automobiles will be ample to meet family needs; prices will remain at about the same levels.

HOUSING, HOUSEHOLD FURNISHINGS AND EQUIPMENT

Mary Jane Ellis
Consumer and Food Economics Research Division

Housing

The housing inventory in this country stood at 58 million units in 1960. At that time the number of households was 53 million. From 1960 until the end of 1963 the net gain to the housing supply is estimated at about 5 million units, the net increase in households at about 4 million. Thus, the current supply allows for some households to have more than one residence and for some shifting of population. But housing is essentially a space bound commodity that must serve a geographically mobile population. As a consequence, at any one time and place the supply may not match demand even though the aggregate number of units exceeds the aggregate number of households.

Construction of new homes.--The annual volume of new housing has increased each year in the 1960's, reaching a total of just under 1.5 million units in 1962. Thus far in 1963 the rate of building is ahead of 1962. May 1963 set a record high for nonfarm housing starts in the 1960's. Only a small proportion of the new construction has been for the lowest income group. Federal, state, and local public housing projects added about 30,000 units to the housing supply in 1962--2 percent of all new nonfarm housing. Public housing starts thus far in 1963 are slightly ahead of 1962.

Single family housing accounted for 73 percent of all nonfarm houses started in 1960-62. The annual building rate for single family houses has been declining, the rate of apartment construction increasing.

More of the new nonfarm housing has been built in the West and South than in the Northeast or the North Central regions thus far in the 1960's. The rate of increase in nonfarm starts has also been greater in the West and South than in other regions. (See table.) Regional data, of course, blur the great differences that may exist among states within a region and areas within a state. Housing starts are not published for individual states. However, Census does provide data on new residential construction authorized in permit issuing places. This building permit series covers about five-sixths of all starts and reveals the geographical pattern in building. In 1962, ten states issued 65 percent of these permits. In order of total permits issued the states were: California, New York, Texas, Florida, Ohio, Illinois, Virginia, New Jersey, Maryland, and Pennsylvania.

Growth in second homes.--Although by no means as common as the second car, the second home is considered to be on the increase. At a trade conference on vacation homes this past spring, vacation homes were estimated to comprise 6 percent of our total housing. Builders anticipate annual vacation home starts of 200,000 by 1970--largely in vacation home developments. The demand is expected to come from couples in their 40's who want a weekend place for their children now and a retirement home later. Apartment dwellers are considered good prospects for developments located not more than 3 hours driving time from the city.

Nonfarm housing units started, by region

Region	1960	1961	1962	1st quarter 1963
U.S. Total (thousands)	1274	1337	1458	293
Northeast (thousands)	236	265	275	34
Share of U.S. total (percent)	19	20	19	12
Change from previous year (percent).	-16	+12	+4	-13
North Central (thousands)	299	281	285	33
Share of U.S. total (percent)	23	21	20	11
Change from previous year (percent).	-19	-6	+1	-15
South (thousands)	425	466	519	126
Share of U.S. total (percent)	33	35	35	43
Change from previous year (percent).	-16	+10	+11	+11
West (thousands)	314	321	379	100
Share of U.S. total (percent)	25	24	26	34
Change from previous year (percent).	-17	+2	+18	+22

Source: U.S. Department of Commerce, Bureau of the Census.

Maintaining the housing inventory.--Maintenance, repair, and improvements that keep existing housing in the inventory cost the American consumer more than $11 billion in 1962. Urban renewal programs are credited with spurring interest in restoring houses of architectural value and in remodeling of other houses. Installment credit has been fairly easy to obtain for home repairs and improvements. The estimated debt outstanding on repair and modernization loans in June 1963 was 14 percent greater than in June 1960, according to Federal Reserve Board reports.

Housing vacancies.--The homeowner vacancy rate was 1.6 percent of the homeowner inventory for the third quarter, 1963. This was the first quarter in the 1960's to show a rate outside the range of 1.1 to 1.4 percent. Vacancy rates in rental units rose from 7.2 percent in the first quarter to 7.6 percent in the third quarter, 1963. This is within the range of 7.2 to 8.1 percent for rental vacancy rates thus far in the 1960's.

Vacancy rates for both owned and rented housing are highest in the West and South, the regions where housing construction activity has been greatest. Like other housing statistics, vacancy rates can be very spotty and vary greatly within states and within parts of a city.

Costs and prices.--Labor costs have been moving upward in the 1960's. Average hourly earnings of workers in general building contracting were 4 percent higher in May 1963 than in May 1962. The Boeckh Index of Residential Construction (including both materials and labor costs) was 2 percent higher in July 1963 than in July 1962.

The housing component of the Consumer Price Index increased 1 percent from September 1962 to September 1963. Rents increased 1 percent; gas and electricity showed no change; solid and petroleum fuels increased 2 percent; and household operation prices increased 3 percent. Prices for housefurnishings remained about the same. From June 1962 to June 1963 consumers also experienced a 1 percent rise in home maintenance and repair costs. Homeowners' property insurance rates increased 3 percent and interest rates on first mortgages declined 1 percent.

Home financing.--From a financial standpoint the American family's opportunities for homeownership have improved in recent months. Federal Home Loan Bank Board summaries of conventional home mortgages (about 75 percent of the nonfarm home mortgage business) indicate a slight decline in interest rates in 1963 and considerable liberalization of terms. The trend thus far in the 1960's has been toward less use of government-backed loans in the purchase of new homes.

Rising foreclosure rates, particularly for mortgages insured by the Federal Housing Administration, have brought warnings from Federal Reserve Board members against lowering mortgage standards, especially in areas that seem to be overbuilt or have high vacancy rates. Foreclosures per thousand mortgages of three types have been as follows:

	1960	1961	1962
All	2.65	3.62	4.12
Federal Housing Administration insured .	3.02	6.29	9.27
Veterans Administration guaranteed	2.89	4.23	5.88
Conventional	2.48	2.77	2.34

Current housing developments in government.--The 1962 executive order concerning equal opportunity in the sale or rental of housing where Federal ownership or operation exists or where Federal financial assistance had been involved has recently been broadened to include provisions regarding fair employment practices by the builder. As of September 1963 only one builder had been suspended from further FHA-VA help because of practicing discrimination in the sale of homes. There seems to have been little real testing of the order. Some builders may be shifting to conventional loans to avoid the antibias pledge. In nine states this would not work since there are antidiscrimination-in-housing laws that apply even though financing is completely private. Eight additional states have antibias legislation that is tied to publicly financed housing. Two states and several cities have gone further in providing rules for the revocation or suspension of licenses of brokers and salesman found guilty of scare tactics to induce panic selling in neighborhoods subject to or undergoing racial or ethnic change.

Developments in construction standards, methods and materials.--During the past year the Federal Housing Administration approved the omission of cross bridging in floor joist spans of 15 feet or less. This does not affect floor strength in the average-size house and will mean reduction in building costs. FHA standards have also been amended to require the use of safety glass in large sliding doors and shower stalls. Safety glass is more expensive than ordinary glass, but this ruling is a safety gain for consumers.

Among new building methods and products designed to reduce hand labor and weather-influenced on-site construction costs are all-steel foundations, factory applied finishes to siding (one carries a 15-year guarantee), prefabricated sections that can be locked into place, molded plastic shower installations, and plastic piping for waste and water lines.

Other new products available are: Vinyl coated steel doors with foam plastic cores that resist warping, keep a permanent finish, and offer better insulation; magnetic weather stripping for effective protection against wind and rain; and a pushbotton water system that controls temperature, pressure, and water flow and is reputed to eliminate leaks and dripping because the lines aren't under pressure. Many anticorrosive, antistain, and water resistant materials are available for items ranging from utility connections, water heaters, and flues to kitchen cabinet surfaces.

Materials developed for commercial building use often have promise for the home: Man-made marble and synthetic brick and slate flooring materials, acrylic window panes, and luminous ceiling installations are examples. Innovations in soundproofing materials and techniques are being adapted for diminishing noise transmission in houses. Window sashes of rigid vinyl and removable plastic grills that give a large window area the effect of many small or diamond shaped panes show promise for easing window cleaning problems.

Outlook.--The building industry is looking forward to a really big boom beginning somewhere between 1965 and 1970, when the World War II baby crop is having babies, bursting out of apartments, and looking for houses. Anticipation of this boom seems to prevent any great concern over increasing vacancy rates, increasing mortgage foreclosure rates, and higher costs of materials and labor. California is expected to continue as the boom area in home building. More emphasis is likely to be on developments of owned vacation homes.

In the more immediate future, consumer prices for housing can be expected to continue their slow upward movement. Mortgage money is expected to be plentiful and terms liberal as to length of maturity and ratio of loan to price, with no great change in interest rates.

Household Furnishings and Equipment

Production levels.--According to the Federal Reserve Board's index of industrial production of goods for the home, production has been generally upward in 1963 and at a higher level than in 1962. Production of black-and-white television sets and home radios lags behind other home appliances, furniture and rugs. Production of color TV sets is reported to be increasing faster than black and white sets.

According to trade sources, early shipments of washer-dryers, floor polishers, wringer and spin-type washing machines, dehumidifiers and chest freezers were smaller this year than in 1962. Shipments of all other major items increased at least moderately. Air conditioners, portable dishwashers, phonographs, vacuum cleaners, and refrigerators went well above their 1962 rates.

Consumer buying.--Buying of furniture and appliances corresponds closely to housing activity. Retail sales of furniture and home furnishings stores in June 1963 were 5 percent above June 1962. Sales in household appliance, TV, and radio retail outlets were 7 percent greater in June 1963 than June 1962.

Users of installment plans now find that downpayments are either not required or have been substantially reduced. Payments for large appliances and furniture at some retail stores may be stretched over 36 months, instead of the usual 24.

Prices.--Retail prices for housefurnishings in September 1963 were about the same as in September 1962. This represents a tapering off in the slight downward movement that has occurred since 1960. As of June 1963 the downward movement was continuing for prices of wool carpets, nylon carpets, and particularly for appliances. However, this was being offset by rising price levels for Axminster rugs, dinnerware, and such small items as paper napkins and electric light bulbs. Prices for television sets and radios declined 2 percent in the year ending June 30, 1963.

New developments.--In kitchen ranges, automatic features are being stressed such as "programmed cooking" in which the product is baked for the set temperature and time, then held at a lower temperature presumably to give some leeway in serving time. One new electric range has an easy-to-care-for oven with removable side and back panels coated with "Teflon." Another cleans its own oven by operating at a temperature of approximately 900 degrees during the cleaning period, thus reducing oven soil to easily removed ash.

Electronic advances developed for guided missiles are being applied to automatic washers. This use of solid state circuitry (incorporated in what the trade refers to as a "little black box") permits a greater range of motor speeds than previously possible (a gentle hand washing action for example). It also means greater reliability and less servicing as well as easier service when it is needed. High cost and other development problems limit use at present, but the little black box should give rise to household appliances much more flexible than present models in the jobs they will handle.

Thermoelectric refrigerators have been introduced on the market recently. There are models for use in the recreation room, the office of a business executive, and the family car.

New items in small appliances are an iron with its own headlight for showing the user where the wrinkles are, and a cordless electric mixer with a rechargeable battery pack that may well be the forerunner of other cordless household appliances. Manufacturers dress up the old appliances in attractive "new" colors or restyle them for buffet table use, as has been done with the hot plate and coffee urn. Radios and phonographs restyling has also been occurring. Record players are turning up in coffee tables and desks.

There has been a big promotion of small screen portable TV sets selling at under $100, produced in competition with Japanese imports. Sales promotion is being directed at the need for a second set and at the teen-age market. Beginning on May 1, 1964, all TV receivers manufactured must be of the all-channel type to permit receiving UHF (ultra-high-frequency) telecasts. Resulting price increases are estimated to be $20 to $30 per set. UHF receiving is much freer from interferences than VHF (very-high-frequency), but UHF does not transmit as far and requires more sensitive tuning adjustments.

Color television is supposed to be ready for the great break-through. Sets were reduced in price this past year and are being advertised by one of the major mail-order houses for the first time. Technical problems in the sets are still a drawback, however, as is the scarcity of color programming by the networks.

Outlook for purchase and prices.--Consumer buying intentions as reported in the quarterly survey in July 1963 suggest that the consumer attitude was slightly more optimistic than it had been a year earlier. Both producers and retailers in the household durables industries were also optimistic and looking for slight gains. Increasing population and increasing income are expected to keep up the market. The increase in the minimum wage effective September 1963 is expected to increase the cost of lumber. However, furniture prices are not expected to advance much.

MEDICAL CARE

Jean L. Pennock
Consumer and Food Economics Research Division

The outlook for expenditures for medical care can be given very succinctly. In the years ahead, we will be buying more medical care and paying higher prices for it. This, of course, can be said of almost all the categories of family living to one degree or another. In the case of medical care, we will be buying enough more, and the prices will be enough higher that medical care will take a somewhat larger part of our total expenditures.

Changes in expenditure patterns, 1950 to date

Average expenditures.--The Consumer Expenditure Survey of the Bureau of Labor Statistics puts urban spending for medical care at an average of $345 per family in 1960. 1/ This compares with $197 in 1950, and is an increase of 75 percent. Department of Commerce 2/ and Social Security Administration 3/ series (which include expenditures for personal consumption made by others as well as consumers) indicate increases close to 100 percent over the same period. We can expect that the Consumer Expenditure Survey data for the rural population will show a greater increase than does the urban data but possibly not as great as we find in the Commerce and Social Security series.

Medical care in the family budget.--The increase in spending for medical care in the last decade was steeper than the increase in total spending for family living. As a result, medical care now takes a somewhat larger share of total expenditures than formerly. Urban families put 6 percent of their total expenditures into medical care in 1960 as compared with 5 percent in 1950 and 1941. This shift is also apparent in earlier data for farm families. Medical care took 7 percent of their total expenditures in 1941 and 9 percent in 1955.

Distribution within the medical care category.--In terms of the ultimate disposition of the consumer's medical dollar--the goods and services he buys without regard to the method by which he buys them--hospital care took 2.6 percentage points more in 1960 than in 1950, moving from 25.6 percent to 27.2 percent of the total. Physicians' services declined approximately the same amount, from 28.5 percent to 26.0 percent. Other changes in all cases were less than a percentage point.

In terms of the way families lay out funds, the big change is in the proportion they prepay--the proportion going into health insurance. The change the Consumer Expenditure Survey will show will be so great that direct payments to vendors of medical goods and services, hospitals included, will be less important than formerly. Information about dollars spent on insurance is not available, but figures on insurance coverage prove this point.

First consider the proportions of the population having any insurance coverage in 1950 and in 1961. The proportion having hospitalization insurance is a fair estimate of the proportion having any insurance, since relatively few persons have other types without also having this type. In 1950, 51 percent of the population had hospitalization insurance; in 1961, 75 percent were covered. Then consider the breadth of coverage. The types of insurance carried in addition to hospitalization give one measure of breadth. In 1950, 29 percent of those covered for hospitalization had no other coverage, 71 percent had surgical insurance also, and 28 percent had medical insurance.

1/ Chase, Arnold E., Bureau of Labor Statistics, Changing Patterns of Consumer Expenditures, 1950-1960. Paper presented at the annual meeting of the American Statistical Association, Cleveland, September 4, 1963.

2/ Currently published as Table II-4 in the July issue of the Survey of Current Business and in the supplements to this periodical, U.S. Income and Output.

3/ U.S. Department of Health, Education, and Welfare, Social Security Bulletin, November 1961.

By 1961, the proportion having no other coverage had fallen to 7 percent, while 93 percent of those insured for hospitalization had surgical coverage also and 69 percent had medical coverage. Important, also, is the rise in the proportion of the population having coverage for major medical expenses. This type of insurance insures the holder to a very high level as to total expense within the year and within his lifetime, and puts little or no limitation on the type of expense. This type was just becoming available in 1950; in 1961, 19 percent of the population had this coverage.

Variability of medical care expenditures.--The year-to-year and family-to-family variation in spending for medical care rather than the size of the average expenditure has made this category a stumbling block in family money management. Medical care expenditures may have risen, but are they as variable as they used to be? Are the minor expenditures of a sizable proportion of families--for little more than aspirin and cold medicines--balanced by a few families spending half or even their whole year's income for the treatment of serious illness or accidents? Obviously with insurance coverage at the level it is today, unless their premiums are paid by their employers, there can be few families with only nominal expenditures. What has happened at the other end of the range can be learned from survey data.

In the 1962 Survey of Consumer Finances, interviewers asked a national sample of spending units whether they had had what they considered large medical expenses in 1961. 4/ Forty percent reported that they had had large expenses. "Large" is a relative term, however, and public discussions of the high cost of medical care may have conditioned the respondents' use of it. More factual information can be gained by looking at the expenditures designated as large. Out-of-pocket expenditures of $1,000 or more were reported by 8 percent and of $500 to $1,000 by 15 percent of those who considered they had had large expenditures. On the other hand, 35 percent reported amounts less than $200. This is considerably less than the average expenditure per family but under some circumstances it may truly be large in relation to other expenditures and to income. Almost half of those who reported having had large expenditures either were completely uninsured (31 percent) or not covered for the eventuality that caused the expense (16 percent).

A further indication of the "smoothing" effect of insurance can be seen in a survey conducted as part of the National Health Survey program. 5/ Among all patients discharged from short-stay hospitals in the 2-year period July 1958-June 1960, 68 percent had some portion of the hospital bill paid by insurance and 51 percent had three-fourths or more paid. Men were more likely to benefit than women. Persons in the middle years (45-64) were most likely to benefit, those over 65 least likely. Only 55 percent of rural farm residents had some part of their hospital bill paid, as against 70 percent

---

4/ Katona, George, Charles A. Lininger, and Richard F. Kosobud. 1962 Survey of Consumer Finances, Ann Arbor, Michigan, 1963.
5/ Proportion of Hospital Bill Paid by Insurance, Patients Discharged from Short-Stay Hospitals. Series B, No. 30, Health Statistics from the U. S. National Health Survey, U.S. Department of Health, Education, and Welfare, Washington, 1961.

of urban and 72 percent of rural nonfarm residents. The greatest variation occurred by income class, those needing the cushioning effect of insurance getting it least. Only 40 percent of discharged persons with family incomes under $2,000 received some insurance payment on their hospital bills, compared with 81 percent among those with family incomes of $7,000 or more.

Factors affecting the Level of Medical Care Expenditures

Price changes.--The medical care index is currently the fastest rising component of the Consumer Price Index. Price change is by no means the whole explanation of the increased spending for medical care, however. Between 1950 and 1962 medical care prices rose 56 percent, while per capita medical care expenditures rose 105 percent in the Commerce series.

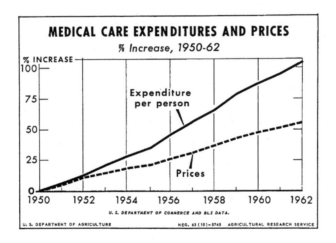

Prices of all types of medical care have not risen at the same rate. Since 1950, hospital rates have shown one of the steepest rises and currently are going up very sharply. The price of hospitalization insurance has risen even more sharply. It appeared to be leveling off recently, but the pressure of hospital rates has forced it up again.

Changing needs.--Another factor that has increased spending for medical care and will continue to do so is changes in the age distribution of our population. Our population is aging, and the need for medical care increases with age. In particular, older people need more of the more expensive kinds, like hospital care. In addition, in the next few years we will have a sharp increase in the number of women in the child-bearing years. In the latter part of this decade we can expect another baby boom of considerable size.

Increased ability to pay for medical care.--In the decade 1950 to 1960 real income rose 35 percent. This in itself would permit some expansion in spending for medical care. The possibility for increased spending is, however, even greater than this gain indicates. As income increases, the pressure to provide food, housing and clothing becomes less severe and other categories can expand their share of total spending. Over the decade the proportion of total spending of urban families taken by food, housing, and clothing in combination decreased, making possible an increase in spending for other categories of family living proportionally greater than the rise in income.

Changing practices and standards.--This is a coin with two faces. On the one side we have had tremendous developments in medical science that tend to push up the cost of medical care. The new drugs, the more elaborate diagnostic procedures, the team approach to the treatment of disease, and the new surgical procedures, all cost more than the old ways. On the other side of the coin is the general public's increasing recognition of the value of spending for medical care. We have been educated to want a high level of medical care and to be willing to pay for it even though we may protest loudly as we pay.

For a measure of this double change in our standards, let us look first at hospital utilization rates. In 1950 out of every 1,000 persons in the population, 110 were admitted to general hospitals (all types other than mental and tuberculosis) and they stayed an average of 10.6 days. In 1960, 136 persons per 1,000 entered hospitals and stayed an average of 9.3 days, resulting in an increase of 9 percent in person-days of hospitalization per 1,000 persons. The 24 percent increase in the admission rate as well as the 9 percent increase in the rate of utilization, increases hospitalization expenditures. Costs are considerably higher in the first few days of hospitalization since elaborate procedures tend to be concentrated there.

Further evidence in the change in our standards regarding medical care can be seen in the change in the utilization of physicians' and dentists' services. In 1928-31, the average person saw a doctor three times a year and less than one person in three saw a dentist within the year. 6/ By 1957-59, we were making five visits per year to doctors and 1.5 to dentists. 7/

New Developments

To counteract the impression that medical care expenses will sky rocket in the years to come, a few developments that will ameliorate the rise can be cited. One is a program that will transfer some of the costs from the individual consumer to the public at large. The Kerr-Mills Act

---

6/ Collins, Selwyn D., The Incidence of Illness and The Volume of Medical Services Among 9,000 Canvassed Families. Federal Security Agency, Washington, D.C., 1944.

7/ Volume of Physician Visits. Series B, No. 19, Health Statistics from the U.S. National Health Survey, U.S. Department of Health, Education, and Welfare, Washington, 1960.

Dental Care, Interval and Frequency of Visits, Series B, No. 14, Health Statistics from the U.S. National Health Survey, U.S. Department of Health, Education, and Welfare. 1960.

provides Medical Assistance for the Aged through grants-in-aid to the States as part of the public assistance program. As of July 1963, 28 States, the District of Columbia, the Virgin Islands, Puerto Rico, and Guam had programs in operation under this act. The State programs vary considerably, but in all the money can be used to pay for care received by recipients of Old Age Assistance and by those able to support themselves except for medical care.

The Administration proposes a somewhat similar program but ties it to Social Security both as to eligibility and financing. There are also efforts to make health insurance more available to those over 65. More than half the employees now covered by industrial group health insurance plans can keep their insurance after retirement, and this feature is being written into a high proportion of new industrial group policies. This, however, will help future more than present retirees. Of more interest to the latter group is the "guaranteed" insurance being offered those over 65 by both commercial insurers and Blue Cross-Blue Sheild. By "guaranteed" is meant that the applicant is accepted without regard to his health status. Premiums for this insurance are higher than for younger persons, of course, but are said to be roughly comparable to plans for the elderly that select only the good-risk individuals.

Efforts to cut costs for all, regardless of age, center around the hospital and its use. There are efforts under way to investigate the abuse of hospitalization insurance and to correct it. To reduce the cost of legitimate use of hospitals, plant and operation are undergoing widespread scrutiny. Efforts in this direction range from the proposed use of disposable sheets to reduce laundry charges to radical redesigning of hospitals. A type of redesigning receiving much attention provides separate areas for patients based on the amount of care they need.

In summary, high grade medical care is part of a high level of living. In as much as we all look forward to a constantly rising level of living, we can expect an increasing outlay for medical care.

Cost of 1 Week's Food at Home 1/ Estimated for Food Plans
at Three Cost Levels, October 1963--U.S.A. Average

Sex-age groups	Low-cost plan	Moderate-cost plan	Liberal plan
	Dollars	Dollars	Dollars
FAMILIES			
Family of two, 20-34 years 2/...............	14.00	19.20	21.80
Family of two, 55-74 years 2/	12.60	17.30	19.40
Family of four, preschool children 3/	21.00	28.00	32.10
Family of four, school children 4/	24.20	32.70	37.30
INDIVIDUALS 5/			
Children, under 1 year	3.10	3.90	4.20
1-3 years	3.80	4.70	5.40
4-6 years	4.50	5.80	6.90
7-9 years	5.30	6.90	7.90
10-12 years	6.20	8.30	9.60
Girls, 13-15 years	6.50	8.80	10.10
16-19 years	6.60	8.80	10.00
Boys, 13-15 years	7.10	9.80	11.10
16-19 years	8.30	11.40	12.90
Women, 20-34 years	5.50	7.70	8.70
35-54 years	5.40	7.40	8.50
55-74 years	5.10	7.00	7.90
75 years and over	4.90	6.50	7.50
Pregnant	6.90	9.00	10.00
Nursing	8.70	11.10	12.30
Men, 20-34 years	7.20	9.80	11.10
35-54 years	6.70	9.20	10.30
55-74 years	6.40	8.70	9.70
75 years and over	6.20	8.30	9.30

1/ These estimates were computed from quantities in food plans published in Home Economics Research Report No. 20, Family Food Plans and Food Costs, USDA. The cost of the food plans was first estimated by using the average price per pound of each food group paid by nonfarm survey families at three selected income levels in 1955. These prices were adjusted to current levels by use of Retail Food Prices By Cities released periodically by the Bureau of Labor Statistics.

2/ Ten percent added for family size adjustment. For derivation of factors for adjustment, see HERR No. 20, appendix B.

3/ Man and woman 20-34 years; children, 1-3 and 4-6 years.

4/ Man and woman 20-34 years; children, 7-9 and 10-12 years.

5/ The costs given are for individuals in 4-person families. For individuals in other size families, the following adjustments are suggested: 1-person--add 20 percent; 2-person--add 10 percent; 3-person--add 5 percent; 5-person--subtract 5 percent; 6-or-more-person--subtract 10 percent.

CONSUMER PRICES

Table 1.--Index of Prices Paid by Farmers for Commodities Used in Family Living
(1957-59 = 100)

November 1962; March 1963-November 1963

Item	Nov. 1962	Mar. 1963	Apr.	May	June	July	Aug.	Sept.	Oct.	Nov.
All commodities	103	104	104	104	104	105	104	104	104	104
Food and tobacco	--	104	--	--	106	--	--	104	--	--
Clothing	--	109	--	--	108	--	--	109	--	--
Household operation	--	107	--	--	107	--	--	107	--	--
Household furnishings	--	96	--	--	96	--	--	96	--	--
Building materials, house .	--	100	--	--	100	--	--	101	--	--
Auto and auto supplies	--	103	--	--	102	--	--	101	--	--

Source: U.S. Department of Agriculture, Agricultural Marketing Service.

Table 2.--Consumer Price Index for City Wage-Earner and Clerical-Worker Families
(1957-59 = 100)

October 1962; February 1963-October 1963

Item	Oct. 1962	Feb. 1963	Mar.	Apr.	May	June	July	Aug.	Sept.	Oct.
All items	106	106	106	106	106	107	107	107	107	107
Food	104	105	105	104	104	105	106	106	105	105
Apparel	105	103	104	104	104	104	104	104	105	105
Housing	105	105	106	106	106	106	106	106	106	106
Rent	106	106	106	106	107	107	107	107	107	107
Gas and electricity	108	108	108	108	107	108	108	107	108	108
Solid fuels and fuel oil	102	105	105	104	102	102	102	103	104	104
Housefurnishings	99	98	99	98	98	98	98	98	99	99
Household operation	108	109	110	110	110	110	110	111	111	110
Transportation	108	107	107	107	107	107	108	108	108	109
Medical care	115	116	116	116	116	117	117	117	117	117
Personal care	107	107	107	108	108	108	108	108	108	108
Reading and recreation	110	110	110	111	111	111	112	112	112	113
Other goods and services ..	106	106	106	106	106	108	108	108	108	108

Source: U.S. Department of Labor, Bureau of Labor Statistics.